Books by Howard Ibach

How To Write An Inspired Creative Brief, 2nd edition

Praise for How To Write A Single-Minded Proposition:

Distilling a brand's value down into a single phrase is perhaps the most daunting task in marketing. Howard's book makes it a little less so with tons of good advice and relevant examples. The book delivers on its title "How to Write a Single-minded Proposition" but just as important, it helps us understand how this concept has evolved since the 1960s and why it's still relevant today. Recommended reading for anyone who writes, reviews or receives creative briefs on a regular basis.

— Sean Duffy, CEO
    The Duffy Agency
    New Hampshire and Sweden

There's something wonderfully clear after reading Howard Ibach's "How to Write a Single-Minded Proposition": most people in advertising need to re-study this topic. I had intended to skim Mr. Ibach's book... It was slender and looked easy to glide through. Then I ran across something I disagreed with. So, I kept reading, mostly to satisfy myself that I could debunk his point. But he changed my mind instead. Which happened a few more times as I kept reading and focused a little harder. By the time I was done, I was persuaded to keep the book handy.

No matter how much the media landscape changes, there is nothing more powerful than a big idea. And the truly big ideas require a single-minded proposition. You may think you already know what that is. Maybe, like me, you could use a refresher.

— Neal Foard
    Executive Experiential Design Director
    Czarnowski
    Los Angeles

Howard Ibach has written about 'How to write a Single Minded Proposition'. Knowing that in my own book *The Anatomy of Humbug* I've posed a fundamental challenge to the usefulness and validity of this approach, he's been gracious — and brave — enough to devote several pages in this short book to a resumé of my arguments. He's been even more brave in asking me to review his text. [...] [T]hank you, Howard, and respect, for inviting a contrary view. You encourage your readers to think for themselves, and I can't wish for more. (Read full review on www.howardibach.com)

— Paul Feldwick, author
  The Anatomy of Humbug: How To Think Differently
  About Advertising
  London

Howard has given those of us who work in this business a gift. And contrary to what people may think, it is not just a gift for creatives, but for our account management and media colleagues, as well as the clients they serve. The reason it is a gift for ALL of us is that it provides the kind of focus that can lead to truly breakthrough work. A clearly articulated single-minded proposition, powered by a true consumer insight is what can make a "Think Different" or "Just Do It" or "Priceless," instead of the forgettable work we mostly see. He makes a compellingly readable case for investing the time and energy upfront that makes the truly memorable possible.

— Marc Williams
  Executive Creative Director
  Chase
  New York

What is the first thing any creative team looks at when they see a creative brief? The single-minded proposition of course. This book provides some terrific lessons, insights and exercises to help agency strategists laser focus their efforts on writing the best single-minded proposition possible. A must read for any ad student or any ad strategist.

— Mark Jensen
   Lecturer
   Hubbard School of Journalism and
   Mass Communication
   University of Minnesota

This is a great read for anyone who believes that tight strategies actually free creatives to do their best work. HTWASMP is loaded with insights and helpful exercises – do the exercises, seriously. Howard is not afraid to let this book be a living document. It's clear he knows this arena will evolve. He's giving you stuff here that is proven to work, but the inclusion of some other ways to skin the cat at the end of the book prove that Howard's dedicated to helping you be your best strategic self.

— Bob Harrison, Creative Director
   Luckie
   Birmingham, AL

How To Write A

Single-Minded Proposition

Five insights on advertising's most difficult sentence.
Plus two new approaches.

Howard Ibach

From the author of the critically acclaimed
How To Write An Inspired Creative Brief

Published by:

Juju Books

Juju Books
Los Angeles, CA

ISBN: 978-0-692-12000-2

Printed in the United States of America

The advertisements and products depicted in this book are copyrighted materials. They are reproduced for educational purposes only under "fair use" provisions of US Copyright law. They are selected at the discretion of the author since they represent principles discussed in this book.

Author photo credit:
Peter Ney Photography
www.peterneyphotography.com

Design by Rubin Cordaro Design

To Dad.
You taught me what it
means to be a plugger.

Table of Contents

> "The single-minded proposition gives everyone focus. It can liberate the creative mind."
>
> — Steve Wehrenberg,
> Teaching Professor & Program Director
> School of Journalism and Mass
> Communication
> University of Minnesota, Minneapolis

> "SMPs work best when clarity prevails over cleverness."
>
> — Claire Hassid, Principal
> Claire Hassid Brand Planning
> Forest Hills, New York

Section I: Where we are

Section II: Where we can go

Introduction

"I think a good single-minded proposition is imbued with some sort of energy. It's 'loaded' language. It's provocative and evocative."

— Henry Louis Gomez
Director of Planning, MARCA
Miami

"It doesn't have to be right the first time. It needs to go through iterations. Let it evolve. Eventually, you have to put a stake in the ground. At some point, you have to rally as a team."

— Nathan Maehren, SVP
Digital at the YMCA of the
Greater Twin Cities
Minnesota

"You need a whole book to explain how to write one sentence?" a family member asked me. He was clueless about what I do for a living, but don't blame him.

The answer, in a word, is " **YES**."

I was just as surprised as he was. I say that without an ounce of irony or sarcasm. To illustrate this point, I reviewed the Word deck for my first book, *How To Write An Inspired Creative Brief*, a text that takes readers through the process of writing the advertising document of which a single-minded proposition (SMP) is but one part. That text runs to over 18,000 words. The text for this book — parsing just one sentence — comes in at just under 16,000 words. I'm certain I could have written more.

If it were so easy to write this *one* sentence, everyone would be doing it, as the saying goes, and you wouldn't need this or any similar book. You might say that everyone is doing it and doing it poorly. I will amend that to say people attempt to write this one sentence, but they struggle.

I made two discoveries as I wrote: First, I reconnected with colleagues, some of whom I hadn't spoken to in almost 20 years, and I was happily surprised at their ingenuity and imagination. No two answers to the questions I put to them are alike. That speaks to the almost countless avenues into the writing of this beasty little line. It also reveals the amount of energy this line requires of the professionals who spend so much time attempting to write a good one.

Second, these conversations, bits and pieces of which are sprinkled throughout the text, confirm a need to focus on the *basics*, which this book lays out for you to review, consider, challenge and add to. More than anything, I want to start a conversation about the SMP in particular, and generally the Creative Brief itself.

3

Not everyone uses the term "single-minded proposition" or, for that matter, believes in it. This fact lays out the path this book will take. **Section I** addresses the status quo, what's generally practiced and accepted about this one box on the Creative Brief. I will take you through five elements of the brief and examine how each one influences the writing of the single-minded proposition: *communication objectives, product benefits, insights, brand personality* and *target audience*. These elements reside in one phrasing or another on most Creative Briefs.

Section II examines new perspectives regarding the SMP's effect on the brief (new to many, but not all). Here I explore the writing and thinking of two people: Paul Feldwick and Lance Saunders. I have met and worked with Saunders. I know Feldwick only by reputation and the book and articles he authored. Their ideas, many would argue, are already at work in our industry.

Who are they?

Paul Feldwick is a consultant, a brilliant account planner, and a protégé of Stanley Pollitt, one of the founding fathers of account planning, the discipline from which Creative Briefs emerged. His book *The Anatomy of Humbug: How To Think Differently About Advertising* is an enlightening and compelling argument for alternatives to proposition-based advertising.

Lance Saunders is a friend and my mentor when I began studying the Creative Brief seriously, in 2007. When I met him he was director of strategic planning at Campbell Mithun in Minneapolis. Today, he is president and chief operating officer at DDB Canada. Saunders proposes that we focus our energies on an *ownable emotion*.

There are others, I am sure, who echo the ideas presented by these professionals. These two, however, succinctly challenge us to higher standards of truth and authenticity, and therefore better Creative Briefs that inspire better creative work.

What follows are the ideas I think about when I read creative briefs. These are the questions I ask. This is the information I want. This is what turns over in my head.

As an educator, I pay attention to the things students ignore, overlook, forget. I know that students, in general, don't do "optional." I learned that the hard way, probably because I forgot that's what I "didn't do" when I was a student myself. So I take those extra steps and explore as many nooks and crannies as I can. I am curious — perhaps the single-most important quality a creative person possesses.

Call me intrepid. Call me obsessive. All writers would be advised to study the guiding principle behind what makes a well-conceived SMP so gratifying when it's done right: clarity.

5

It's such *easy* advice, and so **difficult** to achieve.

1 Why I wrote this book

"Ad agencies tend to be very good at stripping away the nonsense. We have one ear listening to what our client wants, but also one ear listening to what the consumer wants."

— Rob Schwartz, CEO
TBWA\Chiat\Day
New York

"Ask the right questions, and be ready to hear things from your customer that might surprise you."

— Kristina Halvorson
CEO Brain Traffic;
author, *Content Strategy for the Web*, 2nd edition

In 1989, I was a copywriter for a small business-to-business advertising agency in Milwaukee, my hometown.

Two facts about this job stand out and are relevant to my tale. The first is that the shop did not use a creative brief before I was hired. The document was not part of its day-to-day operations.

The second relates to one of its bigger clients, an American manufacturer of turf equipment, one of whose marketing executives I met on many occasions. This executive repeated a phrase I never forgot. He used it every time I, or one of my colleagues, asked this question on a new project:

> "What's the one, most important thing we need to say about your product?"

Almost 30 years later, his answer lingers in my memory and reflects thinking stubbornly pervasive among marketers to this day.

"We don't have just **ONE** thing," he would say. "We have *a unique package* of features."

That's the first, and primary, reason I wrote this book.

single-minded proposition

Search with Google   I feel lucky

The second reason is because when I write about this topic on my blog and on social media it garners more views, comments and shares than any other. If you type "single-minded proposition" into Google, two of my essays tend to show up on the first page. Maybe that's Google's algorithms flattering my vanity. Try it yourself. I'd be curious to learn what you get.

The point is, people in our industry wrestle with the creative proposition. I know it from reading hundreds, more likely thousands, of Creative Briefs over the course of my quarter-century-plus career as a copywriter and creative director. I have come to understand the challenge by writing about the SMP and the Creative Brief for almost 10 years, and now actively speaking about it for almost as long.

So much rests on these few words. The pressure to get it right is significant.

While it's impossible, indeed unfair, to think of the SMP as its own entity that simply resides within the Creative Brief, but is not integral to it, this mini sculpture of words is often an enigma to its writers. This sentence deserves a book of its own. I leave it to you to report whether this one is worthy.

Who should read this book

If you're an inventor, an entrepreneur, a sales person, a marketer, an advertising professional, a student of any of the above, a teacher of any of the above, or generally curious about discovering and communicating the singular essence of a person, place, thing or idea, this book is for you.

If you're an account planner, understand that I am not one of you, and I am not a pretender. I am a former copywriter and creative director who learned from you, studied your Creative Briefs, asked questions, and read your articles and books.

You inspired me.

9

2

A hard question, a simple answer

> "Miles Davis said that the essence of making music is to take one note and make it do the work of ten. That's a description of a good single-minded proposition."
>
> — Richard L. Gant, Adjunct Professor of Marketing New York University, and Chief Experience Officer RL Gant Group Inc., New York

> "Don't just write it. You have to believe it. Is it going to make you engage? If not, trash it and start over."
>
> — Margaret Murphy, CEO and Founder Bold Orange, Minneapolis

Writing a Creative Brief in general, and the single-minded proposition in particular, are exercises in *reduction*. They are about getting to the essence of a product or service. That's why I love to share Albert Einstein's famous challenge:

"If you can't explain it to a six-year-old, you don't understand it yourself."

Substitute "it" with anything — blue sky, love, your *brand* — and the challenge becomes tangible.

If, for example, you work for Nike, you can't just hand a child a pair of sneakers and say, "See? This is what Nike is." That's not an explanation. It's not even a demonstration. She knows intuitively that you put them on your feet. She will know instantly whether or not the pair you gave her is cool. Her body language will be impossible to ignore. But that does *not* add up to an explanation. You have to use words that a six-year-old comprehends. And when was the last time you read a copy of *See Jane Run?*

Now you begin
to see the enormity
of the dilemma
Einstein lays at your
feet — no pun intended.

I had this conversation with a senior marketing person for an internationally renowned musical instrument manufacturer. He told me his kid hears him talk about his product every day. The kid has seen it, touched it, likely tried to play it or maybe even knows how to play it. But the marketing guy confessed the difficulty of trying to explain what that musical instrument is, and why it matters, in words his child knew and understood. This from a guy who lives, breathes and plays his own brand.

LET'S GET SPECIFIC.

Can you explain Nike Air More Uptempo basketball shoes for girls? What is it about this specific Nike product that you can clearly put into words for a little girl so she gets it? You can go out on a limb and assume lots of little girls know exactly what Nike Air More Uptempo basketball shoes *are*. But that's not the assignment, is it?

Because if you can't explain these "old-school kicks," as Nike's website describes them, I have to agree with Einstein that you not only don't understand the shoes yourself, but you're also likely not communicating their "why you should own a pair now ... today ... " to your ideal buyer, who's not necessarily a six-year-old girl. But she might be!

In other words, you could be leaving product on the showroom floor *unsold*.

This is precisely what we're struggling with when we write a single-minded proposition. It doesn't need to be written for a six-year-old. But when you read a killer SMP, you marvel at its

SIMPLICITY.

And so will the creatives who deliver the ideas that sell the product (even though they might not admit it).

Section I:
WHERE
WE ARE

"It had to be based on something true, some truth in the way a consumer behaves."

— J.F. Fournon, owner of
Machin, Trouc and Chose
Paris

"A good single-minded proposition immediately clarifies, elevates. It works as a jumping off point. Creatives start riffing. Everyone puts their lens on it, and they begin to see how it can be a campaign."

— Bonnie Nijst, President/CEO, ZEESMAN
Los Angeles

3 What, exactly, is a "single-minded proposition" anyway?

"It's an argument. It's stimulus for the creative team. It points them in the right direction. The ultimate idea is that it produces compelling advertising."

— Hart Weichselbaum
Consumer Insights & Brand Strategy
The Planning Practice, Chicago

"The single-minded proposition is a leap of faith. It is how the brief writers understand the personality of the brand, understand the story, and define the best action the brand can take at this point."

— Rashad Moglbay, Director of Strategic Services
@Bold, and Managing Partner, Ameya Agency
Beirut, Lebanon

As its name implies, a "single-minded proposition" is succinct. It is a declarative statement or phrase, and it usually shows up on a document called a Creative Brief. *Creative Brief* is not typically a proper noun, but I've decided to make it one here.

A Creative Brief is a set of instructions written for the creative team or teams at either an advertising agency or an advertiser's in-house creative department, whose job is to translate those instructions into sales-generating communications. This document is supposed to be short and concise, although that's not always the case. The best Creative Briefs tend to be short, but even short Creative Briefs can be unfocused.

A single-minded proposition can also take other names:

I prefer *single-minded proposition*, and in this book, that is the term I will use, or its abbreviation, SMP. I won't, however, make this term a proper noun as well. I don't want to be accused of being a helicopter creative. Not everything is special.

So what's an SMP? As an educator, I've learned that one explanation of a concept is often not enough. People absorb knowledge differently. If someone doesn't understand what you're saying, merely repeating it doesn't offer clarity.

This is the definition of insanity:
doing the same thing over and over and expecting different results.

Consequently, on the assumption that a student or colleague will not always fully get my meaning, I've learned to have at least two, often three, unique explanations of the same idea at the ready.

Here, then, are three unique definitions of the single-minded proposition, each one building on the other. If you're an experienced professional, these should confirm what you know. If you're new to the concept, at least one should resonate. I hope all three drive home the point.

Single-minded proposition definition #1: It's the one essential truth about a product or service that consumers care about most. It answers this question: What's in this product for me? It's all the best benefits and insights of your product distilled to their essence, setting it apart from the competition.

Key words to remember: "single," "one essential truth" and "sets it apart from the competition." Single-minded means exactly that: only one idea.

Single-minded proposition definition #2: Imagine you're standing on one side of Times Square in Manhattan. It's 11 p.m. on a Saturday evening, just after all the Broadway shows have let out. It's a sea of people.

On the other side of Times Square, imagine someone who represents the ideal user of your product. What would you say to this user? Or rather, what would you *yell* across the sea of people that would persuade her to buy your product? The answer to this question is your *single-minded proposition*.

"Yell"

Key things to remember: **"Yell"** because it's gonna be loud, and, although I didn't say so earlier, you can't yell a paragraph. Even a complete sentence might be too much. You probably have to find just the right short phrase to make your case under these extreme conditions.

Single-minded proposition definition #3: Have you heard about those people who can fall asleep on a bed of sharp nails? Yeah, I know: How do they do that? The

explanation, it turns out, is rather simple: Your weight distributed evenly across a large quantity of nails means no single nail penetrates your skin. If you're careful, you can recline without injury, and in theory, fall asleep.

19

Now think about a communication with that many messages (or points, since we're already talking about nails). If you make too many points, none will penetrate the clutter of other messages and resonate with your target audience. It becomes information overload, and the target gets no message at all ... or falls asleep out of boredom.

Instead, imagine your communication with a *single point*. Like a bed with one nail right in the middle **(ouch!)**, this focused message will far more likely get through. That's what a single-minded proposition does. A good one, anyway.

There you are, three unique explanations of the single-minded proposition: What's in it for me? The Times Square analogy. And the Bed of Nails analogy.

Some of my more poetic colleagues grow misty when describing the single-minded proposition. I prefer to remain vigilant and clear-eyed. At its best, the SMP inspires big ideas. At its worst, the SMP is convoluted and masks the idea it's trying to reveal.

Rather than infuse it with mythical power, which only sets you up for failure, look at the single-minded proposition as the "first ad." That's how John Hegarty, founding partner of London's Bartle Boogle Hegarty, describes it. So the pressure is on you to do it well.

Remember that the SMP is singular in nature.

It's never two messages, and *absolutely* never three. Only one.

Nor is it the one distinguishing quality the *advertiser* values most. Sometimes advertisers (i.e., company owners, entrepreneurs, anyone or any group that sells the thing) mistake what *they* like for what the *consumer* likes. That's what you call a clearance item.

I cannot emphasize single-mindedness enough, in spite of what my esteemed marketing executive at the American turf equipment manufacturer would have me believe to the contrary.

That's why this part of the Creative Brief is so important. It's also why it's the most challenging set of words to assemble.

It doesn't require eloquence, but rather an up-in-your-grill directness. The SMP demands the precision of, well, someone who writes easy-to-follow instructions. As you will see shortly, a finely honed single-minded proposition is deceivingly simple. In the practiced hands of an expert, the SMP underwhelms and inspires all at once. It brings out the Homer Simpson in all of us.

DOH

My challenge is not to make the writing of a single-minded proposition easy. That comes only with practice, practice, practice.

Follow the advice I present here, and I can, and will, make SMP writing much *easier*. That I can promise.

Recap: Remember these three definitions:

1 The "single thing" that answers, What's in it for me?

2 The Times Square "concise yell" analogy

3 The Bed of Nails "make one point" analogy

Exercise:

Find a table near you. Any table will do. Now, in your head, do this: "Explain this table to a six-year-old." Hint: You have to assemble words into simple, clear sentences. You can't show your six-year-old a picture. (Review *See Jane Run* for remedial assistance.)

DON'T SMIRK.

All professionals practice, especially basics. You're strengthening your intellectual muscle memory.

Practice this activity once a day. At first, it will take you some time. But as you get good at it, the explanation will come quicker. Pick any everyday object to start. Then graduate to abstractions, like "love," "beauty" or "money." Yeah. Those are tough.

What happened to that smirk?

4. Where does the single-minded proposition come from?

"Talking only to the people who use the product is myopic. Most important, you must talk to people who don't use the brand. You ask, 'Why not?' Those answers also lead to inspiration."

— Tim Holmes, VP
Group Account Director
Martin Williams, Minneapolis

"A good single-minded proposition takes a 12-lane highway down to a one-lane road."

— Reid Holmes
Group Creative Director
Ogilvy/The Lacek Group
Minneapolis

I keep a stash of SMPs rolled up in a little baggie hidden in my sock drawer. Where do you keep yours? If wishing made it so.

It doesn't appear by magic, yet it requires a kind of alchemy.

The process is not a formula, but there is a logic to it.

The SMP rests to the right of an "equal" sign, but it is more than the sum of its parts. A well-written SMP crystalizes the best of an inventory into a short, insightful idea.

The best single-minded propositions I've encountered are deceivingly simple. Yes, you read that earlier in this text. You'll likely read it again. Tattoo it on the insides of your eyelids. It's worth remembering. When an SMP you write produces this precise reaction, you've arrived.

But like the fan of an accomplished athlete who makes a swing, throw, volley, chip shot, layup or field goal appear effortless, we can be fooled into believing we, too, could easily do it.

Unlike the accomplished athlete, the SMP is not the product of a solo effort. Nor should it be. Ad agencies revolutionized creativity in the 1960s by putting copywriters and art directors together as teams. Two heads are better than one. This principle ought to apply to writing the Creative Brief, and especially to the single-minded proposition. You always need a trusted sounding board.

25

Some single-minded propositions are so clever, they end up as brand taglines, public-facing language that becomes embedded in popular culture. Let's take a look at a few:

a) Just do it.

b) We're #2. We try harder.

c) When it absolutely, positively has to be there overnight.

d) The milk chocolate melts in your mouth, not in your hand.

e) A diamond is forever.

f) You get your fresh, hot pizza delivered to your door in 30 minutes or less — or it's free.

g) Dogs rule.

h) AARP gives you the power to make your own rules.

i) The GS300 is the kick-ass Lexus.

j) Toro makes the tools. You make the lawn.

k) Think different.

l) Now you have an expert on your side.

Do you recognize them? Most did not use a product name in the line. Were you able to figure out the brand? Which ones were *not* public facing? The answers are on page 31.

(I would argue that one of these lines is not truly singular in focus. In fact, it contains three ideas. Which one am I thinking of? Do you agree?)

A typical Creative Brief contains a short list of requests, sometimes in the form of questions. The finished brief should fit on one page, at most, two. A progression of content leads up to, but doesn't necessarily conclude with, the single-minded proposition. Nevertheless, the SMP is the *point* of the brief. It's why the brief was written.

Therefore, my aim is to provide you with the shortest, most effective route to the SMP. Typically, this sentence results from or combines *five essential ingredients* of the Creative Brief (many planners would argue that there are more than five mineable veins, and I would not disagree).

The first ingredient appears on every Creative Brief:

communication objectives.

Second, I'll examine ideas that rarely show up verbatim on the brief, but their importance is an integral part of it: **product benefits**.

The third is an **INSIGHT**, which could be about the consumer, the brand category, the marketplace, or a combination of the three, since they are closely linked.

The fourth is **brand personality or character**. When little differentiates your brand from a competitor's, or when your brand lives and breathes solely by the persona identified with it, your brand's personality can be all you need to inspire a single-minded proposition.

Fifth is your **target audience**. The people who use your product or service will always present you with a clear path to a compelling advertising message.

In other words, the brief gives you the flexibility to write an SMP from the strongest, most powerful position at your disposal. But you have to do the work.

27

Creative Brief nomenclature can, and often does, vary from template to template, but the goals should stay the same. What I call "communication objectives" might instead be a question: "Why are we communicating?" Please don't feel bound to use my terminology.

Oddly, sometimes the order of the items on a Creative Brief isn't summative. I have read Creative Briefs that *begin* with the single-minded proposition, followed by its justifications, a deductive way of thinking. That approach pleases the creatives who look for the SMP before anything else. To me, it's an abstruse method. I'd prefer to see the argument of the Creative Brief unfold in a logical, linear manner. (I know, that's not exactly what you'd like to hear from a former creative. I'm in danger of losing my "rebel" badge.)

These ingredients — communication objectives, product benefits, insights, brand personality and target audience — come together and reveal the single-minded proposition. Most well-written briefs, in my experience, seamlessly connect one or more in a unique mix.

The alchemy I spoke of earlier, however, influences each project differently. Sometimes, the SMP is more heavily weighted to the communication objectives. Sometimes the product benefits are more important. Sometimes an insight is so compelling, it takes center stage. Sometimes the brand personality is so dominant or embedded in the culture that it hands you the SMP. Always, always, always your SMP intimately connects to your best customer.

In other words, the SMP is an enhanced version (when alchemized creatively) of whatever the context your project demands. You must be aware of these ingredients and decide based on the market situation — the problem you are asked to solve — which one plays the most influential role.

Throughout this book, I've chosen sample Creative Briefs for familiar products to demonstrate what I mean.

Recap: The SMP doesn't appear by magic, yet it requires a kind of alchemy. The process is not a formula, but there is logic to it. The SMP is more than the sum of its parts.

Exercise:

Think of a brand you work for or use regularly. What's its tagline, its public-facing brand promise? (Think: "Just do it" for Nike.) Which one, or combination, of the five ingredients of the brief does it seem to emerge from?

_____

_____

_____

_____

_____

_____

_____

_____

_____

_____

_____

(NOTE: You may need to guess at this right now, so consider reading ahead and returning to this question. But either way, this is another exercise you "practice" once a day, in your head, about any brand you have even a passing familiarity with. We're honing, baby! We're honing!!)

What I point out in the next pages is how one ingredient, in combination with two or more other ingredients, creates a clear pathway to a single-minded proposition. It's like a team effort. There is likely a single "star," one element that seems to take center stage, but that star stands on the shoulders of a support network we call the Creative Brief.

Answers to questions on Page 26

a. Nike

b. Avis

c. FedEx

d. M&M Candies

e. De Beers

f. Little Caesars Pizza

g. Pedigree Dog Food

h. AARP

i. Lexus (brief only)

j. Toro (brief only)

k. Apple

l. H&R Block (brief only)

Little Caesars Pizza's SMP contains **3** ideas.

5

The point of the communication: objectives

> "The single-minded proposition is the easiest and most compelling reason why I should entertain getting into a relationship with you."
>
> — Neal Foard
> Executive Experiential Design Director at Czarnowski
> Los Angeles

> "I think about the best politicians, the ones who know how to stay on message. The single-minded proposition is not just about your product. It's also about your brand and about all the people who are part of the organization. So no matter who you ask, inside or outside the company, they'll say something similar about the product."
>
> — Nathan Maehren

This is where you begin. This statement, or perhaps it's a question, belongs on every brief, ideally one of the first items.

Identify a short list of tasks — two, three tops — the communication must accomplish. This list will depend on the nature of the communication. If you have the physical space (e.g., email, website, blog post, direct mail, collateral), three tasks are not difficult. If your space is limited (e.g., mobile, print, TV, billboard), you may opt for only one or two tasks.

In *How To Write An Inspired Creative Brief*, I advised you to use verbs for this part of the brief. I called them the John Wayne of words: They're all about action. I grew up watching The Duke on Saturday mornings. A more relevant analogy today might be a cartoon superhero like Wonder Woman or Black Panther. Whoever conjures the image of a "person of action" for you, this is precisely what you want from readers/listeners/viewers of your communication: to do something! Go online, visit the store, pick up the phone, subscribe.

> #1 on About.com's "Ten Advertising Books You Absolutely Must Read"
>
> How To Write An
>
> Inspired Creative Brief. 2nd Edition
>
> Howard Ibach

Communication objectives translate into a call to action. It makes sense, then, for the Creative Brief writer to use *verbs* to accomplish this.

33

For example, here's the Creative Brief for Tango, a soft drink in the U.K.:

TANGO Creative Brief

Brand Proposition	Tango is a sleeping giant.
What do we need to do?	Increase sales of Tango. Re-inform people of our traditional brand values. Reengage people with the Tango brand. Generate key interest in the product.
What are the MARKET insights?	The carbonated drinks market is in decline. Few brands are surviving, and those that are still suffer a drop in sales. This is a result of the media making health a real issue. What was once seen as a passing fad, is here to stay, and in order to stay afloat, brands need to address this health issue accordingly. Tango has always been a controversial brand. It stands out, makes a statement, stands for something. Has the potential to make a statement. Sadly, in recent years, this controversial stance has somewhat lessened. They've gone a bit soft with Tango Clear, and Tango as a brand has virtually fallen off the radar. We need to assert what we are in order to shake up the market and reclaim our prime position.
What are the CONSUMER insights?	Stuck in an in-between state, teenagers associate themselves with the products and brands they consume. They take on a brand's personality as a representation of their own. Therefore, if a brand has no personality, it's impossible for them to feel an affiliation towards it. Tango is definitely a brand with a personality. Sadly, the personality isn't currently being asserted, therefore isn't out there for the taking. In order to gain a loyal consumer base, we need to give them something that's worth being involved with.
What is the single most important thing to say?	# Join the Tango resistance.

Reasons to believe	Tango is not your ordinary drink. It says something about you. It's controversial, daring and overt. This isn't just a carbonated drink. It's a chance to take a stance against the things that hold you back.
What do we want them to do?	Get excited about the Tango revolution and join the resistance.
What do we want them to think/feel?	Think: "Tango understands us."
	Feel: More inclined to drink Tango on a regular basis as it's about more than just carbonated drink
Why would they bother?	This is about them. It empowers them and gives them a voice.
What worked last time?	Tango enjoyed the most success when it was assertive about what it stands for.
Where will this appear?	Integrated campaign with a particular concentration on online as this is where our audience spend most of their time.
Inspirations	Think about what you were like when you were 16.

Look at the second box on the left. It reads: "What do we need to do?"

The first answer is rather obvious: "Increase sales of Tango." It's the weakest part of this otherwise stellar brief. No one's perfect.

Now look at the answers:
• Re-inform people of our traditional brand values.
• Reengage people with the Tango brand.
• Generate key interest in the product.

Notice how each objective starts with a verb, a request for action. Creatives get this. Heck, everyone gets this. This "always use verbs" technique allows you to focus on *what* to say and not *how* to say it. It gives you a vocabulary you can always rely on.

35

Each answer/objective is a command. They are three separate tasks, but each closely relates to the others. In fact, if you examine them carefully, you have essentially two objectives: 1) get people excited, and 2) remind them ("re-inform" and "reengage") about the brand.

MY ADVICE? If you choose to address three objectives in a given communication, make your life a little easier. Always include some version of "Re-enforce the brand" as one of the objectives. Every communication must accomplish this anyway.

Let's take a look at our Tango brief again. The second box asks, "What are the MARKET insights?" The summary: First, soft drink sales are in decline. Second, while Tango had a bit of a rebel brand image, it's gone quiet recently.

One of the reasons I love this brief is that it offers a second insight. This one reads, "What are the CONSUMER insights?" I'd love to know whether every brief Tango's ad agency wrote takes this approach.

Here, the insight offers a challenge: Teens struggle to find an identity, so a brand with personality helps them figure out who they are. Tango needs a personality infusion to give teens a reason to consume it.

Remember, this insight is a challenge, not a prescription. It dares creatives to find a solution rather than handing them one that may or may not work.

(The most common complaint I hear when I lead workshops is about marketers and advertisers who are creative "wannabes." When I became a creative director, the first lesson I required myself to practice was judge the work, guide it from good to better to great, and mentor, but don't do it yourself. That's why you have a staff. This requires trust and big dose of confidence on your part.)

Now we arrive at the heart of the Tango Creative Brief: the single-minded proposition. It's phrased differently on this brief.

"What is the single most important thing to say?"

The answer?

"Join the Tango resistance."

(This is a great proposition. But where did it come from? I'll return to that in a moment.)

What comes next? While I and many call them "product benefits," this brief makes such benefits even more personal: "Reasons to believe." Another way to say this is, "What is the proof that the SMP is true?"

Proof, or reasons to believe, means product benefits.

Let's take a quick detour and review basics.

6

The benefits of product benefits

"You have to dig to find the single-minded proposition. Digging takes time. These days, products are not highly differentiated, which makes the work even harder."

— Claire Hassid

"Know that it's got to be simple. We tend to overwrite, overthink. I want clarity before poetry."

— Rob Schwartz

Do you know the difference between features and benefits?

Veterans roll their eyes. Rookies squirm.

I ask this question because the evidence suggests that too many of us do *not* know the difference. How do I define *too many*? One. That's too many.

Here's my evidence: a billboard for Viagra, or rather, E.D. medication. This is a classic example of a creative team asleep at the wheel. And the creative director. And the account person. And the client. Am I forgetting anyone?

This is a feature-focused ad. There isn't a hint of product benefit here. I've seen this happen many times.

"Wait a minute," you say, puffing up in righteous indignation. "The benefit is, you know, um ... an erection."

No. It. Is. Not.

E.D. is medical lingo for erectile dysfunction. E.D. medication gives the guy who takes it a woody. Thus the (hee-hee) vertical billboard. Unfortunately, that's the feature of the product. All E.D. medications do the same thing: give a guy a hard-on.

But it's *not the benefit.*

"So, professor, what is the benefit?"
you ask.

I should be asking you. If a guy takes an E.D. medication and the pill works, he gets aroused. How does he feel? No, not horny.

He feels like a man again. He's got his groove back. He's feeling like himself, at long last.

That's the benefit. One or all of those reactions describe the product benefit. It's *emotional*. And that's why this billboard is *bad advertising*. It's not a billboard for *Viagra*. It's a billboard for the *category of E.D. medications*.

Oops. I call that a real boner.

"But my client loved it!" you claim.

Uh-huh. What's your point? Do you want to sell your brand or all of them? Do you want to pander or challenge? Do you want to live in the world of lowest common denominator, or take people out of their comfort zones and startle them, engage them, persuade them? One requires features, the other benefits. One is easy. The other is hard(er).

Look at the other Viagra ad below. It's a clever use of type behind the man's head. You see the effect. And the line *brands* Viagra: "Get back to mischief." Have you seen this treatment? Me neither. I think it scared the client. Too bad.

 Now you understand why I feel compelled to review basics. LeBron James didn't become LeBron James because he waited until game time to practice his jump shot. Right?

Back to Tango.

What are its product benefits? We have to do a bit of sleuthing because, quite honestly, I've never tasted it. The soft drink is marketed in the U.K. and Europe. The brand is also known more for its quirky, award-winning advertising.

Blackcurrant, for example, is among its few flavors, along with apple, orange and cherry. It's described as a "piquant berry," which means a sharp, tart or zesty flavor. They add sugar to sweeten it, and other ingredients. But aside from describing its unusual taste (at least to American palates), there's not much else to say.

Enter the power of branding. You make a leap from limited or abstract brand features and make a claim.

That's exactly what this brief does so well. What is the "benefit" of an unusual flavor? Tango claims, "It says something about you. It's controversial, daring and overt ... It's a chance to take a stance against the things that hold you back."

No matter what you think of the taste, you'll love what it does for your ego.

Here's an example of an SMP that the writer derived from a combination of one of the communication objectives, one of the insights (specifically the consumer insight) and the target audience. And what about brand personality? Did that influence the thinking behind the SMP too? Absolutely. If you know your "brand archetypes" (see Chapter 9), you can easily identify which one suits Tango:

OUTLAW.

Which communication objective did it meet? My answer: Tango is an existing brand that needed some energizing. The project was not as much about trumpeting its benefits as it was in re-connecting with people already familiar with the product. In order to accomplish that task, the insight about teens who appropriate a brand's personality to help them figure out their own was keenly observed. Put the three together and the result was creative alchemy: Stand out by resisting the status quo. (This, by the way, is how I answer the question "where did it come from?" I posed, and put off, on page 24.)

41

Note that I'm drawing conclusions from the brief alone. I did not meet the brief writer or interview her, nor was I privy to market research. I'm simply doing a close reading of the document in front of me.

Recap: Communication objectives require *verbs*. Review the difference between a product's features and its benefits, because you need to practice!

Exercise:

Find an old creative brief you wrote at least six months ago. Older if you have one. Locate the text that asks something like, "Why are we advertising?" or "What are the objectives of this communication?" Did you answer using verbs anywhere?

I ♥ Verbs

If so, pat yourself on the back. If not, how could you reword your answers to start with verbs? Which verbs would you pick? The cool thing about verbs is that your language has tons of them. We even tend to make them up. So there's no excuse for not having a bunch to choose from. You can absolutely find the perfect match.

动词

kev hais lus

verbo

verbe

briathar

folje

verbi

verbum

глагол

43

7

What's in it for me?
A different path to the SMP

"The best lines truly come from real life. We are human beings, so it must be authentic."

— Margaret Murphy, Minneapolis

"The SMP is, without a doubt, the most important collection of words on any creative brief or job description. It's the guiding light for the whole project. It's the North Star. In short, it's the foundation on which every great campaign is built."

— Paul Suggett, *thebalance.com*
Creative Director, Starz Entertainment

What if your task is different than Tango's? What if you want to launch a new product or expand the market of an existing product? What if you're talking to a new audience who doesn't know your product? How do you arrive at a "deceivingly simple" but effective SMP?

Use the **product benefit** route. And now that you're reacquainted with product benefits, let's take a look at a relevant brief for Red Bull.

Red Bull didn't give us wings to fly; it grabbed us by the jugulars and sent us soaring.

Red Bull

Background / Overview:
America received her wings in 1996, when "bulls balls" were introduced to the beverage industry. Red Bull focuses on bringing dynamic energy to all realms of life, let it be Nascar, extreme sports, study habits, etc. In that, Red Bull created a niche market based around "energy enhancing beverages." With its "wing enabling powers," Red Bull is considered a "youthful drink" that speaks solely to the youth...until now.

What is the objective, the purpose of the ad?
To expand Red Bull into the older adult market as a beverage that can give them the focus needed to tackle their deepest desires.

Target audience: who are we talking to? What do we know about them that can help us (insight)?
Middle-aged men and women reaching the "midlife crisis" aspect of their lives. They are in need of an internal change and lack the motivation and direction to make it happen. They feel they have wasted away their lives and fear only doom lies ahead.

What's the single most important thing to say? What is the big idea?
Get your balls back.

What are the supporting rational and emotional 'reasons to believe and buy?'
Red Bull increases performance, increases concentration and reaction speed, improves vigilance, stimulates motivation, and makes you feel more energetic and thus improves your overall well-being. About 5%-12% of middle-aged people experience a midlife crisis. They have fears and anxieties about growing older, and are willing to try new and adventurous things to reach a sense of internal stability in their lives.

I like this Creative Brief: It's concise, it's gutsy, it's informative. While it's not perfect, it's easily fixable. It's also missing some important items, so I'm going to assume there had been a page 2 with a few more details (e.g., brand tone, approvals, budget, tactical recommendations, mandatories). This is the brief as I found it.

My biggest complaint is that "target audience" and "insight" are combined. Why? The author rightly asked two separate questions, but wrongly lumped the answers together. The result is that the insight is buried. That's a mistake.

I also question the validity of the insight. More precisely, I don't like its phrasing. This brief was likely written by someone with no idea what a midlife crisis is. C'mon: "They ... lack the motivation and direction to make (a change) happen"? I'm trying not to take this personally. Clearly I'm not the target consumer.

This claim is too broad. If it were narrowed to say, "The 5% to 12% of middle-age men and women who experience a midlife crisis ... are the ones who may lack the motivation and direction ...". Now that's focused and believable, based on the facts listed in the last item of this Creative Brief. Not every middle-age person is helpless.

Aside from this kerfuffle ...

Let's move on to communication objectives. This brief asks a question:

"What is the objective, the purpose of the ad?"

Notice the verbs.

"*To expand* Red Bull into the older adult market ..."

"... *to tackle* their deepest desires."

I would have written this as two short sentences to emphasize both objectives. You see there are, in fact, two objectives here, not one. But that's perfectly okay. These two objectives are closely linked: **expand** in order to **tackle**.

Is one more important than the other? Let's consult the brief:

"What is the single most important thing to say? What is the big idea?"

This is the single-minded proposition, posed here as a question. Notice, again, it asks two questions. Two entirely different questions. Some argue the "big idea" is the goal creatives arrive at, inspired by the Creative Brief. Others argue the SMP can be so clever, so insightful, so definitive, that it is the big idea, and the job of the creatives is to execute it.

I see it both ways. However, I also believe very few SMPs qualify as a big idea all by themselves. Typically, a killer SMP is more inspirational than definitive. And I would prefer this brief asks one question: "What is the single most important thing to say?"

The answer: **"Get your balls back."**

Which of the two stated objectives does the SMP address?

The second: "... to tackle their deepest desires."

Is it addressing both men and women, as stated in "Target audience"? Well, that depends on whether you take the SMP literally or metaphorically. I'm pretty sure they mean the latter.

One thing we can say for certain: This is not public-facing language. A tagline it will never be.

But this SMP addresses the target's perceived problem: difficulty in facing a midlife crisis. And it relies on product benefits to get there. How do we know this?

Take a look at the last item on the brief:

"What are the supporting rational and emotional 'reasons to believe and buy'?"

A close look at the answers provided on the brief tells you: this is a list of product *benefits*.

The key product *features* in Red Bull, as I see them, are the caffeine, vitamin B-12 and vitamin B-6, all recognized as performance enhancers. (Do a quick Google search to verify these nutrition facts.)

The list of claims (increases performance, increases concentration and reaction speed, improves vigilance, stimulates motivation ...) are the benefits. The brief does not provide evidence for these claims, but then this is advertising, not a double-blind laboratory experiment.

Do you see the direct line between these product benefits and the SMP? A single can of Red Bull gives you all these performance enhancers, therefore your midlife crisis is on its way out the door.

Two cans, stand back.

Three cans ... **call 9-1-1**

Recap: SMPs are the result of nuance. While my argument is that you can trace a line from benefit to a single-minded proposition on the Red Bull Creative Brief, the SMP has many mentors.

Exercises:

Stand up. Look at the object you're sitting on (bean bag, recliner, your squeeze). Name two of its features (facts). Identify a benefit for each feature/fact.

Pick an everyday item every day and devote two minutes to practicing this exercise. In 30 days, you'll have a new, valuable habit. And not too far down the road, a

RAI$E

8

Eureka!
The SMP inspired
by an insight

"In the end, it's not about what we think about our brand. It's what your customer thinks. This is the homework part that too many marketers are lazy about doing."

— Tony Hart, Chief Strategic Officer/Founder
StrataScape Consulting, Ltd.

"It was always amazing to me that you could distill hundreds or thousands of inputs about a product — features, benefits, research, competitive insights — and translate all that into one simple statement. This statement becomes the foundation of your advertising program."

— Jeff Perkins, CMO Parkmobile, LLC, Atlanta

Ah, the Holy Grail of the Creative Brief: an insight. Another name for it is "a truth." I'd go further and describe it as an *emotional* truth. A believable, authentic truth will, by its nature, be anchored in an emotion.

If the single-minded proposition is the hardest line to write in a Creative Brief, an insight certainly appears to be the most elusive. A powerful insight is the stuff of which Cannes Lions, and a few other such aspirational goodies, are made. I have my own thoughts on this mysterious beasty.

Because it's not so mysterious. And it's not so elusive, either. But like gold, you must dig for it.

THE RICHARDS GROUP CREATIVE BRIEF
People don't like ads. People don't trust ads.
People don't remember ads.
What will make this one different?

Why are we advertising?
To encourage men to think more about the state of their shoes and what that says about them.

Whom are we talking to?
Men who take pride in their look and feel that their appearance is a direct reflection on themselves.

What do they currently think?
"It's important to look my best on special occasions, but I can get by on a day-to-day basis without my shoes looking great."

What would we like them to think?
"I never realized the statement my shoes make about me. If others are going to judge me by my shoes, I need to do something about it."

What is the single most persuasive idea we can convey?
Though you might not be looking down, others are.

Why should they believe it?
Shoes are a detail that says a lot about you. Kiwi shoe polish helps ensure that your shoes are saying something good.

Are there any creative guidelines?
Brand personality: fun and a bit irreverent.

Take a look at the Kiwi shoe polish Creative Brief by The Richards Group. I categorically love this brief. I love the template itself, and I love the answers. They are short, to the point, informative, inspirational. I especially love the opening exhortation: "People don't like ads. People don't trust ads. People don't remember ads. What will make this one any different?" That warning gives every brief writer pause.

This brief writer (I hope beyond hope it was a *team* of brief writers) stepped up.

My claim in this chapter is that an insight is often inspiration for a killer single-minded proposition. I think this brief provides a good example. Let's look at both closely.

First, the single-minded proposition for Kiwi shoe polish: "Though you might not be looking down, others are."

Wow. That's some serious emotional baggage. Your blissful ignorance has consequences, pal, say the people at Kiwi.

Where did this "argument" come from?

And where on this Creative Brief are they hiding the insight? Because no content addresses it directly.

I see both the origins of the argument and the insight. Do you? The third question sets them up: "What do they [the blissfully ignorant, scuffed-shoe-wearing slackers] currently think?"

The answer, according to The Richards Group, is this: "It's important to look my best on special occasions, but I can get by on a day-to-day basis

without my shoes looking great."

Again, wow. These guys acknowledge they want to look good, but laziness sets in when it comes to their shoes. This is the argument, found within the current thoughts of our ideal Kiwi shoe polish consumer. But we haven't yet crossed the bridge to a truth. This isn't the insight.

The next question delivers the knock-out punch: "What would we like them to think?"

The answer: "I never realized the statement my shoes make about me. If others are going to judge me by my shoes, I need to do something about it."

Ah-ha! Looking good means *all of me*. These otherwise fastidious fellas fail to fathom the fate of their feet fashion (that was fun, wasn't it?).

But hold on a sec. If these slackers were so blissfully ignorant about their shoes, how did the brief writers manage to arrive at this astute insight? How did they make this leap? One minute, sloppy shoes were perfectly okay, and then, voila! They're not acceptable. What happened?

Back up to the brief's second question: "Whom are we talking to?"

Answer: "Men who take pride in their look, and feel that their appearance is a direct reflection on themselves."

How did someone figure out that guys who forgo shoe polish would wake up to this oversight?

I don't have the exact answer. I don't know if the agency had research or piles of relevant data at their disposal. I don't know if they conducted focus groups or did surveys.

What I do know is that, short of these measures, brief writers have a path to an insight like the one on the Kiwi brief. They, and you, have alternatives to paid research.

My favorite option is what I call an "insight immersion." Another term for it is the Socratic Method. In other words, it's real old-school. It's nothing more complicated than a laddering system that asks one question over and over until you arrive at a believable truth, or an insight.

Here's how it works: Begin with the most important benefit of your product. For Kiwi shoe polish, that benefit is stated in the box that asks, "Why should they believe [the SMP]?"

The answer reads, "Shoes are a detail that says a lot about you. Kiwi shoe polish helps ensure that your shoes say something good."

My argument in this chapter is that the *insight* about Kiwi shoe polish inspires the single-minded proposition, not the product benefit, which is an avenue to the SMP I discussed earlier. Therefore, we're using the benefit only as a springboard to the insight.

With this benefit, slightly revised — "Kiwi shoe polish helps ensure that your shoes say something good about you" — you can ask your first question:

"Why is that important to you?"

Now you begin the Socratic process of digging for a truth. What's going on inside the head of this slacker dude who doesn't believe his scuffed shoes make him look bad?

Your first answer might be:

"Because looking good gives me confidence."

Keep going.

"Why is that important to you?"

"Because when I'm confident, I'm more productive."

"Why is that important to you?"

"Because when I'm productive, I feel secure in my work/relationship."

Continue with this line of questions until you arrive at a believable, authentic truth. You might keep going until your answer becomes absurd, no longer believable. Then it's just a matter of returning to the previous, most authentic answer.

You should not conduct insight-immersion research by yourself, however. You need reliable, trusted feedback to test the believability of your answers.

In this particular case, I don't think you'd actually land on the exact wording of the Kiwi brief's single-minded proposition. 55

That doesn't matter.

I think you can see that the SMP on this brief is grounded in a believable emotion: fear. The fear of not looking your best among people whose opinions of you matter: your boss, your colleagues, your family.

Chip and Dan Heath, in their *New York Times* bestselling book, *Made to Stick: Why Some Ideas Survive and Others Die*, note that this "Why?" technique has other iterations. They cite the Five Whys. I have also heard about the Three Whys.

I recommend you ask the question "Why is that important to you?" as many times as you need to. When you work with one or two other colleagues, your combined experience and intuition will serve as effective B.S. detectors, as long as you also remember to test your answers outside your small group. Always test!

Here's one ad for Kiwi shoe polish based on this Creative Brief. What do you think?

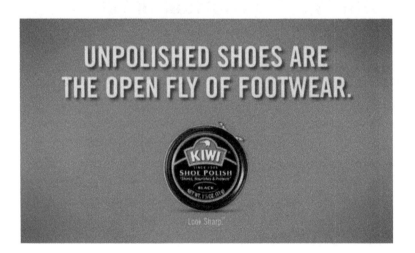

Recap: An insight is invaluable, but it doesn't have to cost any more than the price of a cup of coffee and the time it takes for you and a colleague or two to engage in a Socratic dialogue.

Exercises:

I use Palmolive Clear dishwashing detergent. I like it because it appeals to my minimalist aesthetic. The feature: clear liquid. The benefit: It projects my style.

Now, what "insight" can you arrive at based on this admittedly subjective benefit? Answer the question "Why is that important to you" until you land on an authentic, believable truth.

You can do this exercise every day. Do it with any favorite brand in your world. I urge you to work with a colleague so you have a trusted B.S. detector, someone who can validate your statements.

9

An SMP is born from brand personality

> "We ask our clients to do a Hemingway six-word story exercise to describe their brand."
>
> — Aaron Keller
> co-author of *The Physics of Brand* and co-founder
> Capsule Design, Minneapolis

> "A good single-minded proposition is seeing the truth (about your brand) that nobody saw before."
>
> — Utymo Oliveira, Group Strategy Director, BETC
> Sao Paulo, Brazil

Who is your favorite actor? Your favorite athlete? Your favorite entrepreneur? Think of anyone with a celebrity status, an outsized talent, or charismatic hold on one's imagination, and you understand the power of personality.

Now think of your favorite brands. A few of mine are Disney, Nike, Apple. Which human characteristic fits each?

Imagination? Disney.

Perseverance? Nike.

Cool? Apple.

(It might be worth noting that one of these iconic legacy brands owns a tagline [or brand promise] that began its life on a Creative Brief as the single-minded proposition. Which one? "Just do it," for Nike.)

The point I want you to remember in this chapter is that your favorite brand fits neatly into one of a dozen "brand archetypes," and I've included a list for your review (below). Can you identify the ideal personality of your brand?

Nike, appropriately, is a "hero" personality. Why? Is Nike like Black Panther or Wonder Woman? Sure, that works. But instead, think of Nike as a heroic personality because it steeps its owners in hero-like qualities such as resilience, doggedness, steadfastness and perseverance. When you wear or use a Nike product, you believe you can "Just do it."

Which, I suppose, characterize Black Panther and Wonder Woman, too.

Brand personality can be a logical and powerful catalyst for a single-minded proposition. Let's take a look at a Creative Brief that demonstrates this idea.

CLIENT: BBC

NATURE OF JOB

One off ad / **New campaign** / Press / TV / Ad in existing campaign / Radio / Poster / Cinema

SIZE/TIME — LENGTH

The requirement is to produce the "Big Idea" that will work across TV, Interactive TV, Radio, Online and Broadband

WHAT DO WE HAVE TO SAY?

The Olympics is made of heroes.

WHO ARE WE TALKING TO?

The hearts of every man, every woman and every child.

HOW DO WE CONVINCE THEM (RATIONALLY OR EMOTIONALLY)?

There are 10,500 athletes at the Olympics, with 10,500 unique stories behind them, each a version of the universal Olympic story from the elite-of-the-elite to the athletes from countries with teams of one or two. The blood, sweat and tears, character, the joy of success, setbacks and failures, the people around them, luck and fortune make up the tests and the human story behind the athlete that we can all identify with — the story of a Hero's Journey.

From these moments come the magical moments we can identify with the ones that make up our memories and the excitement of the Olympics. This is why the Olympics can resonate with our deepest emotions and send a tingle down the spine.

TONE OF VOICE

Epic, universal, inspirational, magical, thrilling, spine tingling

This is another ad agency Creative Brief. The shop is **DFGW** (Duckworth, Finn, Grubb and Waters), a London-based agency founded in 1989 and bought by Publicis Group PR agency Freud Communications in 2007.

Take a close look, because this brief is deceiving. Notice the client's name: BBC, as in the British Broadcasting Corporation, the United Kingdom–owned news service.

Now look at the single-minded proposition. On this brief, it's located after the question "What do we have to say?"

The answer: "The Olympics is made of heroes."

So, if you were sitting in a comfortable chair and this brief dropped out of the sky into your lap, and someone asked you to interpret it, you'd have to think a moment.

The client is the BBC, but it's *not* the BBC. The ad agency wrote this Creative Brief *for* the BBC in response to a request *from* the BBC to create a "New Campaign" *by* the BBC to promote the Olympics *on* the BBC in anticipation *of* the BBC's broadcast coverage of the Olympics in the summer of 2012. But the BBC is not the client. *The Olympics is.* (Yes, I know I overdid it on the BBC part, just to be clear).

We're not looking at this brief's SMP for its reflection of the BBC brand personality. We're looking at it for its reflection of the Olympics brand personality.

You still with me? This is what I meant when I warned you about the potential deceptiveness of this brief. It's an excellent one, by the way: It is both brief and creative. It fits neatly on one page and is well written. But it is also not a brief for the BBC brand directly.

You may not know the Olympics' brand personality, but you can guess. And I'll help you by citing from the Olympics official website:

> **"OLYMPISM IS A PHILOSOPHY OF LIFE, EXALTING AND COMBINING IN A BALANCED WHOLE THE QUALITIES OF BODY, WILL AND MIND. BLENDING SPORT WITH CULTURE AND EDUCATION, OLYMPISM SEEKS TO CREATE A WAY OF LIFE BASED ON THE JOY FOUND IN EFFORT, THE EDUCATIONAL VALUE OF GOOD EXAMPLE AND RESPECT FOR UNIVERSAL FUNDAMENTAL ETHICAL PRINCIPLES."**

"The goal of the Olympic Movement is to contribute to building a peaceful and better world by educating youth through sport practiced without discrimination of any kind and in the Olympic spirit, which requires mutual understanding with a spirit of friendship, solidarity and fair play."

Which leads me to my point: Do you see how this brief's single-minded proposition springs from these two paragraphs about the Olympics? These 99 words define a personality: a way of thinking, behaving — living — based on the human qualities of joy, respect, ethical principles, friendship, solidarity, fair play.

What do they add up to? This edges into the subjective, but I think it's fair, more than fair, to say that the young people who compete every four years demonstrate heroic attributes.

You might even say that the single-minded proposition of every Creative Brief that could be written for any media company promoting its coverage of every Olympic Games from now until the end of time is — "The Olympics is made of heroes." DFGW earned its fee on this project.

If there's such a thing as a definitive single-minded proposition inspired by a brand's personality, this one qualifies. You can even hear the official Olympics music in your head as you read it.

You getting a little misty? Me too.

Recap: Your brand has human-like attributes and fits into one of several "brand archetypes." As your brand's guardian, you must know which one and let that guide your work for the brand.

Exercise:

On car trips when I was a kid, we used to play "Find the Beetle." When you saw a VW Beetle, you yelled out,

"Bug!"

Okay, it sounds crazy, but you can do a version of this game — in your head. Anytime you see a brand, identify its brand archetype and name a few characteristics that fit it. Say to yourself, "Hero!" or "Sage!" or "Ruler!" when you spot a brand that fits.

Make it a game. Your friends will think you're nuts, but you're working on your next promotion.

PRACTICE, PRACTICE, PRACTICE!

10 Your target audience will show you the SMP. Just ask!

"Go into consumers' living rooms. Listen to their conversations. Get to know them better, intimately. Knowing the product is easy. Doing a deep dive into consumers' lives is harder. You have to do that personally."

— Rich Russo
Chief Creative Officer/Managing Director
Adrenaline—a Havas Company
New York

"The real secret about a good single-minded proposition is to find out what it is about your product that lends itself to making you feel part of a shared community. We want to be members of a tribe. Passion for a brand is stimulated by a sense of community."

— Neal Foard

You simply can't write a single-minded proposition if you don't know who you're talking to. I mean *really* know this person, inside and out, intimately.

You are not the target, even if you have a month's supply of your brand in your closet. You can't make an SMP work if you're ignorant of the people who use your product.

Which means that, in addition to adopting the arguments I've made up to this point, you must always include this ingredient, this influencer, into the mix of how our sample brief writers arrived at their single-minded propositions. I addressed this directly in the Tango Brief, but nowhere else. It's now time to consider the target's power in developing the SMP.

Let's go back to the Olympics/BBC brief and confirm my observation. Who's the purported audience? (The hearts of every man, every woman and every child.) I love how this brief answers the question. It's not a person or even a mix of people. It's a human organ: the heart. And not even an actual heart, but a metaphorical one. That works!

Typically, when I talk about the BBC/Olympics brief in my workshop, I object to seeing an answer that consists of only a single line. It doesn't do what I like to see when I read the answer to the question: "Who are we talking to?" I want the brief writer to draw a word picture. But on this brief, I make an exception. It's such a succinct line — idea — that I don't need more. As a creative, I love this! It's enough.

Refer to the other briefs: Red Bull, Kiwi shoe polish, even Hush Puppies (see next chapter). Each one demonstrates a familiarity with its ideal consumer, or in the case of Hush Puppies, an unclear knowledge, to compose a compelling, single-minded proposition. Hush Puppies' SMP is the exception.

(The BBC's simple, single line illustrates a fundamental requirement I expect from every brief writer: Show me you can write. You must truly be a *writer*. Someone who loves sentences, who can tell a story. *This skill is an absolute must.*)

Every advertising professional I spoke with said the same thing, if not the same way, when I asked where they find the inspiration for a good single-minded proposition: the target. They all offered other sources of inspiration, often surprisingly original, but sooner or later, each one came back to *the target*.

11

How to fix — or better yet avoid — a bad single-minded proposition

"Look to comedy. Comedy is truth, and that's what a good single-minded proposition achieves. The reason you laugh is because you've never heard it that way before. The joke is an insight about human nature."

— Reid Holmes

"Work with your creative team. You must truly be collaborative so that you develop ideas together. It's really great when a creative brief comes out of collaboration. Creatives are smart. They get it. They can help you come up with a proposition that drives compelling advertising."

— Hart Weichselbaum

This is the hardest phrase or sentence to write on a Creative Brief. Remember I told you the best SMPs are "deceptively simple" creations? Ah, you remembered.

Chances are, if your SMP is weak, the rest of the brief suffers, too. A weak or unclear SMP is a disease infecting the whole.

Unfortunately, bad briefs are everywhere. We've all seen them. Maybe you've written one yourself

(c'mon, be honest!).

This book prescribes a cure to this dreaded malady. So let's apply my soothing ointment to a less-than-stellar brief, and test my remedy.

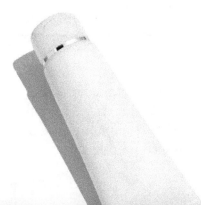

The brief here, for Hush Puppies, is by no means the worst I've ever read. Take a moment to review it. Make note of what you think are its weaknesses, and start thinking about ways we can fix it.

Hush Puppies'

HUSH PUPPIES BRIEF
ADT/001/IMC
Group-5(M2)

BRAND STATEMENT

The Hush Puppies is a lifestyle brand that provides shoes, eyewear, watches and clothing for both men and women.

PROJECT BACKGROUND

Hush Puppies history is rooted in innovation from inventing the first truly casual shoes to developing technologies that make the shoes more comfortable, lightweight and worry free. The brand strives to constantly evolve Hush Puppies world renowned comfort, bringing customers the most advanced technologies available in footwear today. The project consists in developing an advertising marketing campaign of the Hush Puppies shoes that provide comfort and relaxation just by wearing them, because these characteristics are invaluable and enables them to find one more reason to relax.

TARGET AUDIENCE

Males and Females between 20 - 40 years where the audience should be belonging to ClassA, ClassB and chunk of ClassC whose rate of life requires: comfort, functionality and style. People wearing these shoes should need to feel natural, relaxed, authentic, with a young spirit, free, simple and healthy.

ADVERTISING OBJECTIVE

New campaign to increase brand awareness and demand of the Hush Puppies shoes.

CONSUMER MESSAGE

Shoes made as per your lifestyle and choices.

KEY CONSUMER BENEFIT

Provides comfort, functionality and style that touches the lives and imaginations.

BENEFIT SUPPORT

- Whether it is water, stain and scuff resistant *WorryFreeSuede*, or the newest exclusive technology, *WaveReflex* featuring extreme flexibility and technologies like *Zero G*, *Bounce*, etc. Hush Puppies strives to provide benefits that enables to find one more reason to relax.
- Dual-density foam footbed with contoured arch for better grip and elegant shoe designs.
- Handstitched and Environmental aware products.

COMPETITION

AllenCooper, LeeCooper, Blanca, NavyFont, RedTape, Adidas, Nike, Puma and others(as well as other premium Bata product lines too is a setback).

ADVERTISING TONE

Trustworthy, Comfortable, Durable, Modern, Innovative

ADVERTISING MEDIUM

In-store & Outdoor Advertising, Magazines Advertisement and Social Network Advertisements.

MANDATORY ELEMENTS

Hush Puppies Logo, Real Product Image, Attention drawing Text or TagLines, Price and Technology(s), Values and Benefits, Availability(retailers,online & physical stores), Company Website.

This is why I have a hard time acquiring Creative Briefs from my buddies in the ad agency world. Once they figure out I'm going to review and critique their briefs — crickets. I get it. These are not public documents. In fact, they can be considered proprietary.

What do you think? Needs work, doesn't it? Do you agree that the entire brief is weak, not just the SMP? The writing itself is the weak link. It's not clear or succinct. It reads like a hastily compiled first draft. Oh, hell. Let's be honest: It's scary sloppy.

I'll start with specific critiques and then consider some fixes.

The **Brand Statement** is more like a *Bland* Statement. Why is it here at all? It adds nothing to the party. In fact, it projects the message that this brief, while short, is not focused on a style of shoes, or even one line of Hush Puppies' product. Rather, it blankets every product made by Hush Puppies. I'm nervous already.

Project Background. Here's the cause of my nerves: The first sentence tells me the brief is about shoes.

"Project background" is an important part of any brief, no matter where in the document it appears. This paragraph, however, sounds too much like ad copy rather than concise, informed product information. I'd like to see this section focused on something specific. What's the current marketing situation? What's the marketing challenge?

"Background" information can often provide the brief writer with an opportunity to include an insight or little-known product detail. I see neither here.

Target Audience. This tells me nothing about a real human being. Draw a word picture of who buys Hush Puppies. Make this person, or more likely, two or more segments, come to life.

"Males and females between 20–40" covers a lot of people. Your typical 20-year-old likely has vastly different tastes and aspirations than your typical 40-year-old. This category needs more focus. It's too broad.

What is "CLASSA," CLASSB" and "CLASSC" anyway? This kind of business jargon usually has no place on a Creative Brief. I can see an exception for certain product categories (business-to-business, for example), where you might include technical terms. Use your judgment. I try to err on the side of simplicity. Even if everyone knows what these terms mean, a Creative Brief must be the dictionary definition of clarity. You don't want your doctor speaking to you in arcane, undecipherable medical terms, right? Don't commit that sin here if you have better alternatives.

Advertising Objective. I'm getting the sense that this brief is for a campaign to promote the entire Hush Puppies brand, not just one specific style of shoes. So it's not bad. The verb is clear: "... to increase." The task is to increase brand awareness and therefore brand demand.

Consumer Message. This is the single-minded proposition. What do you think? I'd say it's weak. It's redundant: "Lifestyle" and "choices" mean the same thing. This sentence is not an argument. It takes no stand nor stakes any ground.

Would it pass the Sir John Hegarty test? Write "Shoes made as per your lifestyle and choices" above or below a photo of a Hush Puppies product. Is it at bare minimum a good ad? (This was Sir John's criteria.) I don't think so. It doesn't reach high enough to achieve the level of good.

How can we fix this line? Do we know enough to make it better? Not really. I dug around and uncovered two taglines for the brand, but I don't know which one is still in use. Maybe neither. One is: "Free to be casual" and the other, "Shoes you can live in."

74   These lines are important because each is a brand promise. Each one makes a claim about the brand. The absence of such a branding statement on a Creative Brief is a major omission.

If you look at the bottom of this brief, you'll see "... attention drawing text or tagline ..." under the category of "Mandatory Elements." This puzzles me. Shouldn't you actually *write down* the tagline?

For now, we don't know enough to rewrite the SMP. Let's continue our review.

Benefit Support. Hmm. I see a list of product features that only hint at benefits. I can draw some conclusions about *WorryFreeSuede*, but I'd prefer the writer explain it concisely. *WaveReflex* has crossed the line into jargon, although "extreme flexibility" helps some. But then the writer loses me with "... technologies like *Zero G*, *Bounce*, etc." *Etc.*? Seriously?

Although I dislike bullet points anywhere on a Creative Brief, at least these bullets contain seeds of information. But that's not enough. For example, the second bullet, "dual-density foam footbed with contoured arch ..." explains the benefit of "better grip" and "elegant shoe designs," but not very well. Not at the level of clarity a Creative Brief demands, or that creatives deserve.

"Handstitched and Environmental aware products" describes features. What are the benefits of these two facts? It's the job of the brief writer to present this information.

Are these features present on one Hush Puppies shoe model? Some of them? All of them? It's not clear.

Competition. Part of me reacts by saying, "holy shiitake mushrooms." This is some serious competition. My next reaction is, this Creative Brief is not about a particular shoe, it's about the brand. Every shoe they make!

I want more specificity. All of these competitive brands produce multiple shoes, and Hush Puppies isn't competing with all of them. (Is the Layton Genius sneaker going up against Nike Air Jordans?)

My next issue is the general awkwardness of the writing here. I'm inclined to believe this was written as a student project by a student (I *hope* it was written by a student ...).

If in fact Hush Puppies competes with all these brands, the brief writer must provide detailed information about the specific shoe or shoes from each brand. You never see a Ford trucks ad versus a Dodge trucks ad. You *will* see a Ford F150 versus a Dodge Ram 1500 ad. It's not brand versus brand. It's model versus model.

Advertising Tone. The five word choices look as if they were picked up directly from the Hush Puppies brand guidelines. Some parts of a brand's guidelines should reside in a well-composed brief. This is one of them. Well done.

Advertising Medium. One can forgive the brief writer for omitting specifics here. He may not have conferred with a media planner. This document looks dated, too. Today, brands use social media to tell stories rather than run brand ads. Still, this part of the Creative Brief gets a qualified thumbs-up. It could be broken out with more details, but it gives the creative team some parameters.

Mandatory Elements. Wow. Imagine trying to squeeze all this on an in-store point-of-purchase (POP) display. Or a billboard. Or on Twitter. When your Creative Brief requires this kind of information, you must spell out in detail which details belong on which media, paid or unpaid. Yet another reason why this reads like a first draft.

What would you fix? Remember: It's easier to destroy than to create. This isn't a failed Creative Brief. It has potential. With polish and collaborative input, this brief could be stellar.

It lacks specificity, clarity, and a stake-in-the-ground claim. In other words, a single-minded proposition with guts. The definition of an SMP is a bold claim no one else can, or does, make. Maybe I'll add that to my other three definitions.

Recap: Never write a Creative Brief by yourself. Always collaborate. Creative work is always conceived in teams. Writing the SMP, heck the entire brief(!), deserves the same approach.

Exercise:

Find a Creative Brief you wrote six months to a year ago. Give it the same treatment I gave this one. Don't pull your punches. **Be brutal**. No one's looking. It's the best way to get better.

Section II:
WHERE WE CAN GO

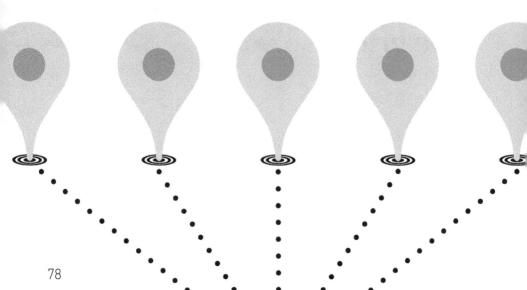

"In the current industry where it's hard to sustain a functional differentiator (thanks to technology), brands opt to create an emotional Unique Selling Proposition."

— Sarmad Hyder
Account Director, Bold Agency
Sao Paulo, Brazil

"A single-minded proposition should be a question. I'd call it the single-minded question. Too many briefs provide solutions and do not ask a question to which you do not know the answer."

— Luke Sullivan, Professor of Advertising and Chair of the Advertising Department, Savannah College of Art & Design; author, *Hey Whipple, Squeeze This: The Classic Guide to Creating Great Ads* 5th edition

"We need to be open to the lessons of [advertising] history in order to deal adequately with the future. Rather than ignore history, or make up simple stories about it, I believe the advertising industry could be both more respectful of its past and more critical of it."

— Paul Feldwick, *The Anatomy of Humbug*

12 A proposition for a new proposition: Feldwick and Saunders

"You have to hear things, to listen without an agenda. I have to 'not know' before I can answer the client's question, 'What should we do?'"

— Bonnie Nijst

"... the more people feel, the more they buy; and the more they feel, the more likely they are willing to pay more."

— Lance Saunders, President/COO DDB Canada, Toronto

The vast majority of industry professionals today subscribe to the "proposition" school of advertising: Establish a rational, singular idea around which to rally, and let the Creative Brief trumpet this promise to creatives. This amounts to the "argument" of the brief, supported by evidence in the form of benefits, reasons to believe, brand personality, insights and target audience. In short, everything I've covered so far in this book.

More and more thoughtful leaders, however, challenge this view. They believe the "proposition" does not address cultural and consumer reality. They aim higher. They advocate for less reason and logic, and more emotion and gut-level thinking: proposition-free Creative Briefs and, therefore, proposition-free advertising.

I agree with this view. The two thought leaders I've chosen — Paul Feldwick and Lance Saunders — bring unique perspectives to what should replace the proposition. Be open to their ideas and their rationales, the logic behind what might seem to be an illogical way into a great Creative Brief and great creative.

In many ways — reflected in existing work — their ideas are an established practice. Gutsy outliers are breaking down old ways of thinking and forcing the rest of us to grow.

As an educator, I am ecstatic. As a teacher of Creative Brief best practices, I am forced to see with "beginner's eyes" and rethink the principles I have taught.

Paul Feldwick

Feldwick became head of planning at Boase Massimi Pollitt and later a worldwide brand planning direct at DDB. He's a 30-plus-year veteran of advertising agencies.

Consider, he asks, these four ads — two print, two television:

The man in the Hathaway shirt

• The eye-patch-wearing "Man in the Hathaway Shirt"

• Commander Whitehead for Schweppe's

• The 1966 black-and-white TV spot for Marlboro

The man from Schweppes is here

• Any TV spot for the Netherlands' Centraal Beheer insurance

If you haven't seen these ads, take a moment to view them on YouTube. Go ahead. I'll wait ... just don't get lost down a rabbit hole.

The first three are iconic, legendary pieces of creative work. The last spots, for Centraal Beheer, have been on air over two decades, and could easily rank among the most creative thinking.

What do they have in common?

According to Paul Feldwick, author of the 2015 book *The Anatomy of Humbug: How To Think Differently About Advertising*, **none of these ads has a proposition**. We could likely manufacture one after the fact, but remember: The first three were created before Creative Briefs existed. As for Centraal Beheer, Feldwick argues:

> **❝** The connection with insurance is slight: each film ends with an unexpected disaster, and the only mention of the brand is in an end frame with the words 'Just call us.' From the point of view of proposition advertising, it makes little sense; indeed, many professionals seeing these films for the first time suspect they must be a bit of pure creative indulgence. Yet the campaign is undoubtedly effective, and has won awards for effectiveness as well as creativity **❞** (147–48).

The argument in *Humbug* begins with a succinct presentation of the history and characters of our industry and the variety of theories of how advertising works, about which, sadly, too many of us are ignorant. To test my point, and his, try this quiz. Raise your hand if you know the following names and can say something factual about each:

- John E. Kennedy (E. not F.)

- Claude Hopkins

- Daniel Starch

- Rosser Reeves

- Ernst Dichter

- Bill Bernbach

- Stephen King
  (no, not that Stephen King)

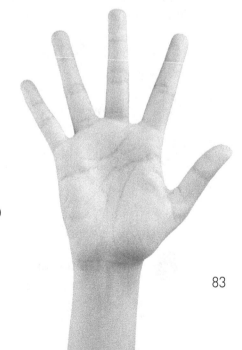

My guess is, if you're a creative, you've heard of Bill Bernbach. If you're an account planner, you may know many, perhaps most, of the names. If you're in account management ... I'm afraid to ask.

Feldwick recites our industry's beginnings, describing the early days of "rational persuasion," and the legends who espoused this approach and wrote books about it. The word "proposition" arrived in the ad lexicon from this perspective. This section, entitled "Salesmanship," opens his book.

Next, the author outlines what he calls a "parallel history of ideas about advertising which locate its effects less in rational persuasion and more in the power of images, symbols, emotions and the subconscious mind." He calls this section "Seduction." In it he discusses the role of motivation research and Bill Bernbach's creative revolution in the 1960s and 70s.

In revisiting two classic techniques — Salesmanship and Seduction — Feldwick suggests how they are both still relevant today, but where "each can be misleading or limiting." He does not reject either entirely.

Then he identifies four additional ways to think about advertising:

1. **Salience**, or fame;

2. **Social connections**, or how advertising is a means of creating and maintaining relationships;

3. **Spin**, or advertising's parallel relationship to public relations; and

4. **Showmanship**, which, by the way, is the source of "humbug" in his title. It's not what you think it means.

Here's Feldwick's definition, influenced by the life and career of P.T. Barnum:

❝ Humbug, as Barnum promotes it, is about shamelessly rigging the odds in your (brand's) favor. It's going with your gut feeling. It's sticking your neck out and not worrying too much what others might think. It believes that there's no such thing as bad publicity. It's not ashamed to be popular, vulgar, even crass. It doesn't take itself too seriously, but it also knows that if it doesn't get enough people in the tent, it won't eat. It's confident and has a brass neck.

"And this principle of humbug fits surprisingly well with much of what has succeeded best in the world of advertising ❞ (159).

He concludes his text by reminding us of a Volvo truck television ad starring Jean-Claude Van Damme to illustrate the relevance of many of the approaches that make up his argument. He sees much at work in this spot. Go to YouTube to review it.

Feldwick claims that any one of the six models he presents could explain this spot. He argues that the rational proposition is "these trucks have superior steering[.]" He goes on to say, "There is a subconscious association — they're tough and handsome like the actor. There's fame — it's just getting talked about ... [b]ut when I saw this commercial, my first thought was — this is straight out of the fairground. It's pure P.T. Barnum. This is pure humbug."

Feldwick proposes gut-level advertising, not something message-less. Ads that spring from rational thinking, where a traditional proposition makes sense, have their place. Instead, Feldwick challenges us to think more expansively. Evidence demonstrates, he argues, that proposition-based advertising creates the least-effective advertising.

This idea may strike fear in the hearts of analytical, corporate America, but it's hard to ignore Feldwick's arguments. He makes a strong case for a new kind of proposition. A proposition based on an emotional relationship between brand and consumer, perhaps based entirely on this emotional relationship.

Lance Saunders

Lance Saunders, president and chief operating officer at DDB Canada, amplifies this conversation about emotion-based communications. In a phrase, his argument is "Facts tell. Emotions sell."

Saunders wrote a brilliant piece for the summer 2017 issue of *Strategy*, titled "Cage match between art and science." He makes a cogent case against the reliance on reasoned, proposition-focused messaging.

His claim is compelling:

"The empirical evidence regarding how we, as consumers, decide to buy is now irrefutable and based solely on emotion, not rationality," he writes. "This is not the ranting and raving of a hungover ECD [executive creative director] in a Cannes breakout salon on creativity. This is brain science. The playbook that we have all used, written in the 1960s by the CPG [consumer packaged goods] giants and focused on the importance of reasoned messaging, is not how communication works — in truth, it may never have worked that way."

In a wide-ranging and impassioned telephone interview, Saunders extends his thoughts:

"I'm not sure that 'proposition' is the right word today," he said. "It seems so dated. It seems like we're trying to sell, but are we trying to sell functionally? Or emotionally? Or something with cultural resonance? I struggle with a 'proposition.' It feels like I'm saying, 'I'll tell you something to sell you something.'"

He continues:

"U.S. advertising is proposition and functionality driven, whereas in Europe and Asia it's not. Advertising is much more about 'entertain me.' If you do, if you entertain me, I may listen to you. I'm reminded of Howard Gossage's line, 'The real fact of the matter is no one reads ads. People read what interests them, and sometimes it's an ad.'

"What we strive for here at DDB Canada is something more visceral. Instead of asking, 'What is the single-minded proposition?' we ask, 'What is the visceral, emotive response we want from this communication?' It could be a few sentences. It could be an entire paragraph. It could be a story. You tell this story to the creative team. It's about how to inspire the creative team. That part of the process hasn't changed. The single-minded proposition is also supposed to inspire creatives. Our visceral, emotive response story must do the same thing. The results are different."

SO WHAT IS THE DIFFERENCE?

"It's not different from what you'd want from a single-minded proposition," he says. "It's just deeper. We started to look at it less from a brand-centric perspective and more from a consumer-centric perspective. Now we're moving further toward a cultural-centric view. We want to know how this brand plays a role in [consumer] lives. How does it address people's hopes and fears? We've become students of the human condition, of society. We're connecting in a deeper way, so we must be well read about culture, behavior, psychology. We've elevated brands to a much higher level."

If you move away from the reason-based proposition to something visceral and emotive, what does it achieve when it's done well?

"It takes off," he says. "It takes on a life of its own. This can be hard for [client] brand managers to understand. Remember that consumers assign aspects to a brand, not brand managers, not clients. Steve Jobs said, 'Your brand is what other people say about you when you're not in the room.'"

"If the visceral, emotive response story is done well, the brand can become news. And when it becomes bigger than you, it's magical."

Finally, I asked him to offer advice to writers of this visceral, emotive story.

"The days when the planner would go off into a room by herself and be immersed in the brand, then emerge with a finished brief are gone. Today, you have to surround yourself with a much larger variety of people, including an account planner. But also your creatives, digital people, journalists, psychologists, cultural anthropologists, people from outside the ad agency. You must have deeper, real conversations about the brand. The process today must be more collaborative.

"You must ask the question, 'How do we want people to experience the brand?'"

Ultimately, argues Saunders in his *Strategy* article, "We need to stop worrying about what is the ownable message, and concentrate on what is the ownable emotion. ..."

His evidence is persuasive. He cites a study called "Marketing in the Era of Accountability," conducted by Adam & Eve DDB's Les Binet, who teamed up with Peter Field. This study analyzed over 800 cases from the U.K.'s IPA (Institute of Practitioners of Advertising) database. The results?

Saunders writes: "In the Binet and Field study, rational-led campaigns performed the worst, delivering big profit gains in only 16% of the cases. Twenty six percent of campaigns that were both emotional and rational had profit gains, while emotional-based campaigns performed the highest with 31% of the cases turning a profit."

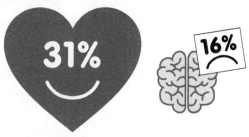

Saunders asks a legitimate question that provokes another: Why do advertisers continue to rely on rational messages in the face of such stark, contrary evidence?

Yes, that's a rhetorical question.

Final thoughts

> "The process is about looking at what everyone is doing so you can do something else."
>
> — Rob Schwartz

> "I look to stand-up comedians. They are always working with the truth and human insights, insights into human behavior, which is where the best briefs come from."
>
> — Luke Sullivan

As I begin the tenth year of my journey as a Creative Brief trainer, advocate, regular essayist on the brief — and "Creative Brief Whisperer," as one reviewer called me — allow me these summarizing indulgences:

First, from the day I began writing about the Creative Brief in 2008, I repeated one thing over and over: The brief is only a template and must adapt to circumstances. That remains true. Today, most brands embrace the necessity of an emotion-driven message, whether the brief utilizes a proposition or something else.

I believe the single-minded proposition still plays a powerful role on the brief and in sparking the advertising that arises from it. Except that it, too, must adapt to be effective.

Creatives expect some focused line that summarizes the direction they must head in, at least in the beginning. Some inspirational nugget. No need to call it a single-minded proposition.

Call it the *unique emotional proposition* — *UEP*. As Lance Saunders suggests, it can go beyond a single line. It could be a story. Allow circumstances to guide you. This should be music to creatives' ears.

Second, the Creative Brief is a *thinking* document. It's not a form to fill out. Forms, like job or driver's license applications, ask you for information you *know already*. All you do is recall the information and write it in the blanks.

Somewhere Aristotle teaches the difference between a "true" question and a "false" question. A true question is one you can't yet answer. A false question, like a rhetorical question, is already known to you.

91

The Creative Brief fits Aristotle's illustration of a true question: You must *work* to find the answer. You must *think* it through! You cannot be what social psychologists call a "think miser" and expect any success with writing this document, much less the single-minded proposition.

Third, some of the most engaging, entertaining creative briefs I've encountered over the years read like narratives. They tell a story, and the writer knows how to keep the narrative moving. Each question or box on the brief stands on its own, which is good, but the overall impression is that you have to start at the beginning, the top of the document, and read it linearly. And you *want* to.

It unfolds with clearly drawn characters (our target), dramatic tension (the business problem), heroes (our brand, our target, insights), supporting cast (the emotional reasons to believe in our brand) and, of course, the resolution (our unique emotional proposition).

Creatives notoriously skip ahead and zoom instantly to the SMP (mea culpa!). But this kind of brief, one that tells a story, simply jars you because you don't read one very often. It stands out. It forces you to **SLOOOOW DOOOOWN**. Now there's a foreign concept in Adland!

Which leads me to my last point and suggestion: Stories demand resolution. We want to know how they turn out. If you write a brief as if you were telling an adventure story, with tension and drama, you cannot help but arrive at the climactic message. I also believe this approach helps inspire creatives to create advertising that tells stories.

If you accept the arguments of Feldwick and Saunders, you also believe in the power of emotion-based advertising, which adds provable selling power to your communications. That emotional engine must be reflected in your proposition, even if you call it by another name.

Some argue that the Creative Brief itself, when done well, is the **BIG IDEA**. Others argue that the brief inspires the **BIG IDEA**. Which camp are you in?

The brief is *step one* in the creative process. In my 26 years as a practicing creative, I learned to trust my creativity and never doubted my ability to arrive at a solution. But I side with the "Brief as the Big Idea." Or rather that it can be, should be, the Big Idea. Too often it isn't, which puts the onus on creatives to save the day. We do. Repeatedly.

It's time for all of us, as a team, to step up — in partnership — and view the Creative Brief and its proposition as the effective result of an essential collaborative process. We all have skin in the game. We all play on the same side of the field.

Acknowledgments

On the theory that there's always someone else to acknowledge, I say "Thank you," even though I may have forgotten to name you here.

I dedicated this book to my father, Harold Ibach. He taught me what it means to be a plugger.

To my sister, Linda Shaunessy, for her invaluable advice and unfailing support.

To my editor, Gail Helland, for clarifying my clarity and energizing my prose. You can never have too much of either!

To my friend and colleague, Tim Holmes, VP, Group Account Director at Martin Williams in Minneapolis, for reading the manuscript and offering cogent, insightful comments, all of which strengthened this book.

To my readers — college faculty, students, advertising creatives and planners, clients — thank you for your supportive emails and inquiries.

To the professional colleagues — and friends — who responded to my request for an interview and who made time for me in their crazy schedules: Kristina Halvorson, Nathan Maehren, Tony Hart, Scott Gilbert, Rick Rosenberg, Rob Schwartz, Bonnie Nijst, Margaret Murphy, Jim Specht, Aaron Keller, Sean Duffy, Lance Saunders, Neal Foard, Tim Leake, Vaughn Davies, Sarmad Hyder, Claire Hassid, Jeff Perkins, Utymo Oliveira, Rashad Moglbay, J.F. Fournon, Richard L. Gant, John Severson, Steve Wehrenberg, Tim Choy, Luke Sullivan, Hart Weichselbaum, Reid Holmes, Henry Louis Gomez, and Rich Russo.

To Jim Cordaro, creative alchemist and designer, and his astute and always reassuring partner, Bruce Rubin, the brilliant duo of Rubin Cordaro Design: my heartfelt thanks and appreciation.

95

And to my literary agent, whoever you are: You'll be thanking me once we meet.

Bibliography

Alda, Alan. *If I Understood You, Would I Have This Look On My Face? My Adventures in the Art and Science of Relating and Communicating.* Random House, 2017.

Boches, Edward. "The insight: The most important part of the brief." *medium.com.* Medium, September 14, 2015. https://medium.com/what-do-you-want-to-know/the-insight-the-most-important-part-of-the-brief-6fb97f6d60d5.

Campbell, Joseph. *The Hero With A Thousand Faces.* Princeton University Press, 1973.

Connick, Wendy. "5 Examples of Unique Selling Propositions." *nasp.com.* National Association of Sales Professionals, Nd. https://www.nasp.com/article/1733F0D9-5C1F/5-examples-of-unique-selling-propositions.html.

Danning, Stephen. *The Springboard: How Storytelling Ignites Action in Knowledge-Era Organizations.* Butterworth Heinemann, 2001.

Feldwick, Paul. *Anatomy of Humbug: How To Think Differently About Advertising.* Tambour Publishing Ltd., 2015.

---. "Account planning: Back to the future?" *marketingsociety. com.* Marketing Society, July 9, 2012. https://www.marketingsociety.com/the-library/account-planning-back-future#1OdHZ2fmBv8xdqMF.97.

Gottschall, Jonathan. *The Storytelling Animal: How Stories Make Us Human.* Mariner, 2012.

Gregory, Alyssa. "How To Write A Unique Selling Proposition (USP). Four Steps To Help You Identify What Makes Your Business Unique." *thebalance.* DotDash, December 17, 2016. https://www.thebalance.com/how-to-write-a-unique-selling-proposition-usp-2951698.

Griner, David. "The Slide that Launched a Thousand Arguments at Cannes: R/GA and Beats tackle the 'numbing consensus' of marketing briefs." *adweek.com*. Adweek, June 27, 2014. http://www.adweek.com/brand-marketing/slide-launched-thousand-arguments-cannes-158630/.

Heath, Chip and Dan Heath. *Made to Stick: Why Some Ideas Survive and Others Die*. Random House, 2007.

Heath, Dr. Robert and Paul Feldwick. "50 years using the wrong model of advertising." *International Journal of Market Research*. Vol. 50, #1. World Advertising Research Center, 16 December 2007. http://paulfeldwick.com/wp-content/uploads/2017/04/Feldwick-and-Heath.pdf.

Hegarty, John. *Hegarty on Advertising: Turning Intelligence into Magic*. Thames & Hudson, 2011.

Ibach, Howard. *How To Write An Inspired Creative Brief*. 2nd edition. JuJu Books, 2015.

Kahneman, Daniel. *Thinking, Fast and Slow*. Farrar, Straus and Giroux, 2011.

Kaufman, Scott Barry. "How Constraints Force Us to Be More Creative." *huffingtonpost.com*. Oath Inc., November 5, 2011. http://www.huffingtonpost.com/scott-barry-kaufman/does-creativity-require-c_b_948460.html.

Millar, Brian. "When I returned to advertising after 10 years I assumed it would have changed—I was wrong." *thedrum.com*. Carnyx Group Ltd., April 25, 2017. http://www.thedrum.com/opinion/2017/04/25/when-i-returned-advertising-after-10-years-i-assumed-it-would-have-changed-i-was?utm_source=Communication+Arts+Daily&utm_campaign=5c10c17ab9-RSS_EMAIL_CAMPAIGN&utm_medium=email&utm_term=0_a6a0e887e3-5c10c17ab9-36024705.

Bibliography *continued*

Perkins, Jeff. "The single-minded proposition." *Ad Age*. Crain Communications, January 21, 2013. http://adage. com/article/btob/single-minded-proposition/288381/.

Reynolds, Garr. "Can limitations and restrictions be liberating?" *presentationzen.com*. garrreynolds.com, March 29, 2007. http://www.presentationzen.com/presentationzen/2007/03/ can_limitations.html.

Saunders, Lance. "A cage match between art and science." *Strategyonline.com*. Brunico Communications, Ltd., July 4, 2017. http://strategyonline.ca/2017/07/04/a-cage-match-between-art-and-science/.

---. Interview. September 15, 2017.

Steel, Jon. *Truth, Lies and Advertising: The Art of Account Planning*. Wiley, 1998.

Suggett, Paul. "How To Use, And Write, The Single-Minded Proposition." thebalance. DotDash, July 20, 2017. https://www.thebalance.com/what-is-the-single-minded-proposition-38457.

Sullivan, Luke. *Hey Whipple, Squeeze This: A Guide to Creative Great Ads*. 5th ed. Wiley, 2016.

Taylor, Alice Kavounas. *Strategic Thinking for Advertising Creatives*. Laurence King Publishing, 2013.

Thompson, Leigh. *Creative Conspiracy: The New Rules of Breakthrough Collaboration*. Harvard Business Review Press, 2013.

Young, James Webb. *A Technique for Producing Ideas*. McGraw Hill Advertising Classics, 2003.

About the author

Howard Ibach is the author of the critically acclaimed graphic textbook *How To Write An Inspired Creative Brief*, 2nd edition, which is ranked No. 1 on About.com's "10 Advertising Books You Absolutely Must Read."

He joined the faculty of the Association of National Advertisers' School of Marketing in January 2017, and travels the country leading workshops that provoke client-side marketers with his radically sane insights on the Creative Brief. He also presents a workshop on mastering the review of creative work.

He was an award-winning advertising copywriter and creative director for 26 years. His specialties were long-form direct response and radio. He worked for legacy shops Ogilvy One, DDB Direct, Wunderman, J. Walter Thompson, and Team One, among many others.

Howard earned his BA from the University of Tampa and an AM from Brown University. He is an essayist, college educator and public speaker. He volunteers at InsideOUT Writers, Inc., a nonprofit organization dedicated to empowering incarcerated youth. He lives in Los Angeles.

Write better briefs in one day.

Howard Ibach's **Inspired Creative Brief Workshop** will show you how to write better creative briefs in a step-by-step process. After his workshop, you will:

- Write tighter, clearer briefs
- Have a new vocabulary for writing creative briefs
- Review creative with more confidence
- Be more confident in directing and working with creative teams
- Be a brand wizard

Here's what others who have attended the workshop have to say:

The **Inspired Creative Brief Workshop** is either a half- or full-day experience designed for account and creative team members. They are collaboration-based interactive workshops that include workbooks, multiple thought exercises and opportunities to write briefs from scratch.

For more information, or to book a workshop, visit

www.howardibach.com today.

CPSIA information can be obtained
at www.ICGtesting.com
Printed in the USA
LVHW011938101118
596544LV00026B/514/P